MW01140295

DIRT AND DESTRUCTION
SPORTS ZONE

MUD TRUCK RACING
TEARING IT UP

BRIAN HOWELL

Lerner Publications Company • Minneapolis

Lerner Publications Company

A division of Lerner Publishing Group, Inc.

241 First Avenue North

Minneapolis, MN 55401 U.S.A.

For updated reading levels and more information, look up this title at www.lernerbooks.com.

Content Consultant: Charlene Bower, Bower Motorsports Media

Library of Congress Cataloging-in-Publication Data
Howell, Brian.
     Mud truck racing : tearing it up / Brian Howell.
          pages   cm. — (Dirt and destruction sports zone)
     Includes index.
     ISBN 978–1–4677–2118–9 (lib. bdg. : alk. paper)
     ISBN 978–1–4677–2452–4 (eBook)
     1. Mud racing—Juvenile literature. 2. Truck racing—Juvenile literature. I. Title.
GV1029.9.M83H69 2014
796.7—dc23   2013022841

Manufactured in the United States of America
1—VI—12/31/13

The images in this book are used with the permission of: © iStockphoto/Thinkstock, p. 5; © Pukhov Konstantin/Shutterstock Images, p. 6; © Robert F. Bukaty/AP Images, pp. 8, 22–23, 25, 28; © Michael Doolittle/Alamy, pp. 8–9; © Frank11/Shutterstock Images, p. 10; © Alden Pellett/AP Images, p. 12; © Kevin Cederstrom/The Minot Daily News/AP Images, p. 13; © Jimmy May/Bloomsburg Press Enterprise/AP Images, p. 15; © Alan C. Heison/Shutterstock Images, pp. 16–17; © Sarah Bates/Anderson Independent-Mail/AP Images, p. 17; © Steve Mann/Shutterstock Images, p. 18; © Zhukova Valentyna/Shutterstock Images, p. 19; © Sascha Burkard/Shutterstock Images, pp. 20–21 ; © Don Ryan/AP Images, pp. 26–27; © Michael Doolittle/Alamy, p. 29.

Front Cover: AP Photo/Keith Srakocic (main); © Janis Smits/Shutterstock.com (background).

TABLE OF CONTENTS

CHAPTER ONE

HISTORY OF MUD TRUCK RACING

A white pickup truck covered with stickers sat on the shallow edge of a mud pit. The engine growled loudly as the driver waited for the race to start. The pickup was ready for a quick race. The truck's big tires would help grip the deep mud track. When the driver saw the green flag to start the race, he slammed his foot on the gas pedal, and the truck took off through the mud. The truck threw mud and water high in the air as it flew through the messy track. The race lasted only a few seconds.

People have been mud racing for decades. The sport combines power, speed, and mud into one race. It started when truck owners, especially those with four-wheel drive vehicles, would try to find soggy, messy, mud pits for racing. Years ago, there were no fans in the stands or prizes to award. Drivers simply wanted to test their truck's limits and get a little messy.

Mud races are only a few seconds long, but the mud flies from the start.

MUD TRUCK TELEVISION

In 2013 more than 20 million homes in the United States had access to *Mud Truck Television*. Started by Brian Austin and his wife, Lisa, the show puts the sport of mud racing on display for fans. The show started on a local cable channel in Arkansas before it went nationwide on the Untamed Sports TV Network.

Mud racing is not limited to one type of vehicle. Drivers can modify other vehicles, such as all-terrain vehicles.

IT'S ALL IN THE TIMING

Mud racing generally features timed events. The fastest driver wins. Since not every driver is able to finish the track, sometimes the winning prize is given to the driver who goes the farthest on the track in the least amount of time. The prizes for mud racing vary at each event. Most races offer small money awards and trophies. Other events have prizes of $5,000 or more.

Fans enjoy watching the unique mud-racing vehicles. They also love the speeds the vehicles travel and the mess they make. When the sport first started, it had few fans and took place only in muddy backyards. It has become a professional sport with national champions.

Mud racing has two categories. Drivers can compete in mud bog racing and fast-track racing.

Mud bogging is when drivers test their vehicle's limits. They drive a set length in a mud pit as fast as they can. The track length varies, but it is always deep with mud and has water on top. The water is about 1 to 2 feet (0.3 to 0.6 meters) deep. When the vehicles speed through a bog, their wheels kick mud high into the air. Drivers race for the fastest time. They also try to travel farther down the track than the other vehicles.

Mud-racing vehicles often become stuck in the mud. They are towed off the track and cannot finish the race.

Side-by-side racing is common for mud-racing events.

Vehicles can get stuck in the deep mud and not make it to the end of the track. Watching vehicles get stuck makes the races more exciting.

To get through the mud faster, drivers began to modify their vehicles. "The cars kept getting faster and faster and faster," Mike Zibella, president of the Mud Racers Association (MRA) said. Drivers' need for speed led to the creation of the fast track. The fast track is an average length of 150 feet (46 m). The track can be up to 300 feet (91 m) long. It is filled with 8 to 18 inches (20 to 46 centimeters) of loose dirt. Organizers add water to create a mud pit. The vehicles tear through fast tracks more quickly than mud bogs.

Two vehicles race side by side in both mud bog racing and fast-track racing. The starting order of the vehicles is by random drawing.

Whether driving through goopy mud or zipping through a fast track, mud-racing vehicles provide much entertainment for fans.

CHAPTER TWO

THE RACES

Mud racing is a popular event for auto-racing fans. The fast trucks, with mud flying in all directions, and the loud engines are exciting. Many people who own extreme cars and trucks enjoy testing the limits of their vehicles. They take them off asphalt roads

WRANA 1

233

One reason mud racing drivers enjoy the sport is because it gives them the chance to test the limits of their vehicles.

RECORD RUN

Mud-racing vehicles are known for their speed. Mike Lane is the fastest mud-racing driver. In 2009 he drove a vehicle named Attitude across the 200-foot (61 m) track in South Haven, Kansas, in just 2.110 seconds. That same year, Mark Lee set the speed record for a 160-foot (49 m) track. In Kanawha County, West Virginia, Lee finished the track in 1.861 seconds.

and into the dirt. Many drivers get their first experience mud bogging in local fields.

Mud racing has grown into a major motorsport. Mud-racing organizations, such as the National Mud Racing Organization (NMRO), MRA, and the American Mud Racing Association (AMRA), organize dozens of races each year.

The 4-Wheel Jamboree National Series is home to NMRO mud bog and fast-track racing. The NMRO events are one of the most popular series of mud races. In 2013 the 4-Wheel Jamboree made stops in Missouri, Pennsylvania, and Indiana. Some of the most exciting events at 4-Wheel Jamborees are the fast-track and mud bog races, but there is much more to see than just mud racing. The events also have monster truck displays and exhibitions. Monster trucks are pickup trucks with big tires and special engines. The trucks race against one another and perform tricks.

The 4-Wheel Jamboree makes stops across the country hosting mud-racing events.

For more than 30 years, the 4-Wheel Jamboree Nationals event has been held in Indianapolis, Indiana. It is one of the biggest events in mud racing. The 4-Wheel Jamboree Nationals crown a new champion in each of six different classes. The classes are based on the types of vehicles used in the races. Some classes require stock trucks, while others require highly modified trucks.

The MRA hosts several races throughout the southern United States each year. The 2013 finals were held in Cobbtown, Georgia. Most of the events scheduled by AMRA take place in Louisiana. Smaller groups also hold mud-racing events across the country.

Mud races are different everywhere you watch them. While the rules may vary, the general atmosphere is the same. Fans, drivers, and

crew members enjoy being at the track. There is lots of noise and excitement. "I still enjoy it," said Mike Zibella. "The people you race against, you become friends with. It's more than just the racing [that makes it great]; it's the whole atmosphere of the event."

Fans enjoy watching the messy sport of mud racing as much as the drivers enjoy making a mess.

CHAPTER THREE

MUD TRUCK MANIA

Mud-racing trucks are some of the most unique vehicles in all of off-road racing. Like all race cars, mud-racing vehicles are built to move fast. Their engines are made with speed and power in mind. Some trucks even have airplane engines. Mud-racing vehicles are

HILL-AND-HOLE RACING

A different type of challenge for mud racers is called a hill-and-hole track. In standard bog racing, goopy mud sits on a flat track. A hill-and-hole track features two hills and three holes. The course is approximately 200 feet (61 m) long. The first hole is usually 12 inches (30 cm) deep. The second hole is 24 inches (61 cm) deep, and the final hole is 36 inches (91 cm) deep. The drivers need to go through the holes, not around them. This slows down their speed. The driver with the fastest time or farthest distance wins the race. In addition to goopy mud, drivers sometimes face unique obstacles, such as logs or rocks, along the track.

Drivers modify their vehicles to be more powerful and faster on a mud-racing track.

built to tear through thick mud. Many vehicles have special tires, allowing the truck to paddle through deep mud with ease.

Mud-racing vehicles in the 1970s and the 1980s were built similarly to today. Many drivers used pickup trucks or sports utility vehicles (SUVs). Drivers would put bigger tires and more powerful engines in their vehicles to help move through the mud bogs. Even after modifying their vehicles, drivers had trouble getting through 2 feet (0.6 m) of mud. The desire to go faster through deeper mud led to changes in the sport and the vehicles.

Mud racers began to use high-performance motors in the 1980s. A high-performance motor helps a truck move through thick mud faster. Many mud vehicles today still resemble those used in the 1980s. The stock classes feature vehicles bought from a dealership, such as Jeeps or pickup trucks.

Other classes of vehicles have taken the sport to a new level. For example, there are classes for modified vehicles. These custom-built vehicles are designed for the sole purpose of mud racing.

Some mud-racing drivers choose to drive Jeeps or pickup trucks. These vehicles are similar to those used when mud racing first became a sport.

Other mud-racing drivers race in custom-built or modified vehicles.

UNITED

Some mud-racing vehicles have a supercharger added to their engines.

Mud-racing drivers sometimes add superchargers to their engines. A supercharger helps the engine create a great deal of power. "[The superchargers] force the air into the engine," Zibella said. "By doing that, it makes the engine make a lot more horsepower."

Another advancement in mud-racing vehicles has been the type of fuel used to power the engines. Years ago, all mud vehicles were powered by gasoline or diesel fuel. Technology has improved over the years, and only stock classes use gas or diesel. Many of the modified and unlimited classes use nitrous oxide or alcohol instead of gasoline. Nitrous oxide provides more oxygen to the engine. This gives a vehicle more energy, power, and speed. When the engine burns more fuel, it helps create power to the wheels, moving the vehicle down the track faster. Alcohol also creates more horsepower than gasoline.

With modifications to the engines and the types of fuel, mud-racing vehicles are more powerful than ever.

CREATING MUD

Preparing the tracks for a race is a long process. Race promoters look for level ground. The area should not have any trees, telephone poles, or other obstacles. Farm equipment is used to dig up the ground and fluff up the dirt. Between 8 and 18 inches (20 and 46 cm) of dirt is fluffed for fast-track racing. Water is then sprayed on the dirt to make it moist. For bog racing, a hole is dug between 2 and 3 feet (0.6 and 0.9 m) deep. The dirt is placed back in the hole and mixed with water until the mud is as thick as pancake batter. The track is maintained throughout the day. For example, water is added to keep the track muddy.

The tires on mud-racing vehicles have also changed over the years. Some of the stock classes still use the same types of tires that regular cars use. The modified and unlimited classes use paddle tires. Paddle tires feature long, thick grooves that allow the vehicle to move through mud, sand, and water at a faster rate of speed. The grooves dig into the mud for a better hold on the ground.

With so many advancements in technology over the years, mud racing looks much different than it did 30 or 40 years ago. It will continue to change as drivers look for new ways to create speed and power.

Special tires called paddle tires are used on some mud-racing vehicles. The tires help the trucks move through the mud better.

THE MAKING OF A MUD TRUCK

ENGINE
Some mud-racing vehicles add superchargers to their engines. This helps vehicles become more powerful.

FOUR-WHEEL BRAKES AND REVERSE
All mud-racing vehicles must have four-wheel brakes. These vehicles must also be able to reverse. If a vehicle gets stuck on the track, putting the vehicle in reverse will help the recovery team rescue the vehicle.

DRIVER SAFETY

Drivers must wear helmets and seat belts. This keeps drivers safe if their vehicle were to roll over and be hit. Some events also require vehicles to have roll bars. Roll bars will keep the driver in the car if it were to roll. Other events require vehicles to have emergency switches so the vehicles can be turned off remotely.

FUEL

Modified mud-racing vehicles use nitrous oxide or alcohol instead of gasoline. This gives the vehicles more energy, power, and speed.

TIRES

Paddle tires are used on some mud-racing vehicles. These tires have long, thick grooves to help move the vehicle through the mud better.

MUD TRUCK RACING CLUBS

Organizations such as NMRO and MRA hold national races throughout the year. They are also responsible for creating many of the rules used in mud racing. Some clubs across the country have adopted the rules set up by NMRO or MRA. Other clubs establish their own rules.

One of the most unique aspects of mud racing is anyone with a driver's license can participate. Some events even allow children as young as eight years of age to join the fun. Mud racing has become a family-friendly sport.

"The thing about mud racing, it's a sport for anybody," said Roger Miles, president of the Overlanders 4x4 Club in Galesburg, Illinois. "It's not limited to people that have a lot of money."

If the sport of mud racing relied only on the national organizations, the sport might not be so popular. National organizations mainly promote big mud-racing events. Smaller clubs throughout the country

Mud-racing drivers do not need professional racing experience. It is a sport for everyone.

are designed to promote the sport locally and give amateurs an opportunity to participate. "If it wasn't for the clubs, a lot of [mud-racing events] wouldn't be happening," Miles said.

Fans want to see vehicles churn through the mud at local events. They also want to try the sport for themselves. Local clubs give fans the chance to mud race.

Club members do not just put on shows, however. Miles said one of his club members owns property perfect for mud racing and allows members to slosh through the mud anytime. "We just go out and play on a Sunday and just have a good time for the day," Miles said.

Most clubs are small operations. The Overlanders 4x4 Club is one of the oldest clubs in Illinois. Miles helped form the group in 1975. Every year the club holds six events. Even with its long history, the Overlanders 4x4 Club has only about 50 members. There might be 400 to 500 spectators at a local event. Miles said that when the club puts on a show at a fair there may be as many as 3,000 to 4,000 spectators.

Some local clubs enjoy mud bogging for fun on the weekends when they are not racing at events around the country.

MEGA TRUCKS

A popular form of mud racing involves mega trucks. Most mega trucks look like monster trucks equipped with mud tires. Mega-truck racing often combines elements of fast-track and mud bog racing. Hills and other obstacles are included in many mega-truck courses.

The West Virginia Mud Racing Association also hosts races throughout the year. The club has six different classes and crowns a champion in each class every year. Each class has certain rules a vehicle and its driver must follow.

VERMONSTER 4X4

Since the mid-2000s, Vermonster 4x4 events in Bradford, Vermont, have been popular in the northeastern United States. With two events each summer, Vermonster 4x4 presents competitions in 10 classes of head-to-head racing. The events also have hill-and-hole racing, deep trenches for mega-truck racing, and challenging obstacle courses.

Drivers and fans both love the mess of mud-racing events. As the sport continues to grow in popularity, more events will be added across the country.

The Vermonster 4x4 is a popular mud-racing event in the eastern United States.

Similar clubs have been formed in other states. The Home Town Mud Racing Association in Utah, Trout Creek Mud Racing in Louisiana, and Concerned Racers 4-Wheel Drive Club in Michigan are just a few examples of clubs that host mud-racing events.

Whether the event is the annual 4-Wheel Jamboree in Indianapolis or a race in a pit of mud in the middle of Illinois, mud-racing drivers and fans always have a good time watching vehicles fly through the mud.

GLOSSARY

ALL-TERRAIN VEHICLE

a small motor vehicle with three or four wheels that is designed for use on different types of terrain

BOG

wet, spongy ground

FOUR-WHEEL DRIVE VEHICLE

a vehicle in which all four wheels are powered by the engine

HORSEPOWER

a unit of measurement used to determine the power generated by a vehicle

MODIFY

to change

NITROUS OXIDE

a colorless gas sometimes used as fuel in mud-racing vehicles

PROMOTER

a person who organizes a public event

FOR MORE INFORMATION

FURTHER READING

Gigliotti, Jim. *Off-Road Racing*. Tarrytown, NY: Marshall Cavendish Benchmark, 2010.

Howell, Brian. *Monster Trucks*: *Tearing It Up*. Minneapolis: Lerner Publications Company, 2014.

WEBSITES

Mud Racers Association
http://www.mudracersassociation.com
This is the official website of the Mud Racers Association organization in charge of mud-racing motorsports.

National Mud Racing Organization
http://www.nmro.net
This is the official website of the National Mud Racing Organization. The NMRO is the head organization of all mud-racing motorsports.

INDEX

ABOUT THE AUTHOR

Brian Howell is a freelance writer based in Denver, Colorado. He has been a sports journalist for nearly 20 years, writing about high school, college, and professional athletics. In addition, he has written books about sports and history. A native of Colorado, he lives with his wife and four children in his home state.